THE NARCISSISM RECOVERY JOURNAL

THE NARCISSISM RECOVERY JOURNAL

PROMPTS AND PRACTICES FOR HEALING FROM EMOTIONAL ABUSE

Cynthia Eddings, LMFT

ROCKRIDGE
PRESS

Interior and Cover Designer: Karmen Lizzul
Art Producer: Sara Feinstein
Editor: Nora Spiegel
Production Editor: Jenna Dutton
Production Manager: Michael Kay

Illustrations used under license from iStock.com. Author photo courtesy of Marissa De La Torre.

Paperback ISBN: 978-1-64876-584-1
R0

CONTENTS

Do the best you can until you know better. Then when you know better, do better.

– Maya Angelou

INTRODUCTION

Welcome to a special healing space. You are most likely holding this book because you are hurting due to a narcissistic relationship. You may be confused, second-guessing yourself, and distant from a person you thought you could depend on. You could also be feeling disengaged from yourself as a result of emotional abuse. This journal is a support you can lean on while you meet yourself in a new way. You deserve to live with a sense of ease, with sprinklings of joy.

If you are under the influence of a narcissist, you may have lost your self-esteem and may be questioning everything about your life. You may be living with feelings of shame, anxiety, frustration, and loneliness. It may be difficult to establish and maintain healthy relationships. Perhaps you're isolated because you don't have anyone in your life who understands your struggle. You might be frozen in what feels like a shameful situation—but the thing is, it's not shameful. You are not alone in waking up to find yourself in a destabilized reality. Narcissism is everywhere. This kind of abuse creeps in seductively and slowly until you look around and wonder how you got in this situation. A narcissist can be a parent, friend, spouse, or someone at work. A narcissist can be any gender. I want you to know that you can start unfreezing while moving toward a better future. This journal listens as you share your pain and your hopes. It becomes a light that will show you where to step as you move out of the dark. My message to you is one of hope. Have you ever asked yourself, *Is there a way out of this stuck place?* The answer is yes. You can become untangled and reclaim your life.

I created this journal because the narcissists in my own life put me on a healing journey, and as a result, I have a renewed sense of self, which supports my ability to live with presence and ease. I now offer hope to others who struggle to find their ground. Through my work as a psychotherapist, my focus is on helping people heal from the damaging effects of narcissism in their lives.

The transformation you long for is private and personal. In other words, your journey is a solo one—but you don't have to go it alone. If your situation requires professional help, there is no shame in seeking help or treatment. This journal is not a replacement for a therapist, medication, or other medical intervention. Resources at the back of this journal can guide you in how to seek professional help.

If I could, I would be sitting with you as you learn about yourself. Since that is not possible, I invite you to call upon your imagination and visualize yourself being held by a wise, loving being as you read and write and explore new possibilities. This wise being is a part of you that you can rely on to be nonjudgmental and nurturing.

Understanding Narcissism

Narcissism is a personality type that's skilled with a sometimes inconspicuous way of knocking you off your feet. Narcissists can have a magnetic presentation of charm, making them impossible to resist. As time goes on, you find you are destabilized in a different way by their unyielding emotional abuse. You once felt close to and safe with them, but now feel defensive and guarded, second-guessing yourself. As a result, you try harder to make things right, but your conversations start to go in circles, and you find yourself desperate to win your narcissist's approval. Anxiety, confusion, and frustration lead to depression. You are now too exhausted to argue, collapsing into the belief that there is something wrong with you. You may be saying to yourself, *They're probably right; I am too sensitive. I am the one with the problem.*

Narcissism exists on a spectrum. You have most likely been managing a relationship with someone on the severe end—an extreme narcissist. This person is incapable of seeing things from any point of view other than their own. Narcissists are addicted to attention. They manipulate to get adoration and obedience, concerned only with their issues, and they disregard authority and rules, thinking these apply to others but not to them. They feel inferior on the inside, so they furiously guard against exposing this vulnerability. Narcissists do whatever they can to feel and appear superior on the outside. They see the people around them as extensions of themselves; therefore, they are triggered to rage if they feel challenged or criticized. Your narcissist has likely been using you as their supply for validation and attention.

If your narcissist is on the severe end of the spectrum, they have wreaked havoc, diminishing your life to survival mode. Emotional abuse leaves little space for you to be you. This abuse may have come in the form of verbal insults, being unavailable if you are in trouble or need help, threatening abandonment, not following through on promises, shaming you, and/or not taking responsibility but blaming you for whatever went wrong. No wonder you are afraid, confused, and don't know where to turn.

If you (and possibly your children) are experiencing physical abuse, such as hitting, victimization with weapons, harm to animals, or forcing or trapping you in any way, call the National Domestic Violence Hotline on page 134 and get help getting out!

So here you are, in a challenging situation. But it offers the treasure of transformation. Your pain led you to this journal, and your experience with it can bring change in the form of healing. Change requires strength, determination, and a shift in mindset. It won't happen overnight. It's a process that builds on itself, and it will provide you with rewards along the way. Hope comes with change. Specifically, the exercises in this journal will guide you to your unique way of adjusting how you think and behave.

It's time to focus on you—finally. Paying attention to yourself might feel uncomfortable and even selfish. It's not selfish—it's your life! You might find that your personal history has made you especially vulnerable to a narcissist's ways. You can stop this pattern and come to know what it feels like to put yourself first, to be whole, to be loved.

Doing the work presented in this journal will bring your soul to life. You'll have something that is all yours. Do it in whatever way you like. You can work through these pages from beginning to end, or skip around to whatever section calls to you. Let yourself be surprised at how strong you are and how much you can learn. You have made a powerful, positive choice to enter into this space. It's time to step in.

**Fall seven times,
and stand up eight.**

—Japanese proverb

Acknowledge and Accept Your Experience

Accepting your reality will help you find your path to empowered well-being. By acknowledging and naming what has happened, you can get some clarity about your situation and gain focus as you start to heal. You are a victim of a damaging relationship.

When you choose to respond to your situation as an opportunity to grow and heal, your perspective shifts to being in the position of having control over your life. Simply acknowledging it will free energy you've been using to avoid your reality, and it's the first step in moving from being a victim to one who was victimized.

The burden of pain is a heavy weight. You might be feeling anxious about facing yourself and the unknown. Acknowledging that you've been the victim of emotional abuse might bring up shame and damaged self-esteem. These feelings are normal, and they will change. Working through this section will help you start becoming a new you.

Your narcissist could be a parent, a romantic partner, a coworker, the person who signs your paycheck, or a friend. Write about how you feel when you're around this person and how you feel when you anticipate seeing this person. For example, you might feel anxious when you are about to see this person. Or maybe you feel guarded, like you're walking on eggshells. Perhaps you are angry whenever this person is around. What's it like for you?

Excited to see them and recieve validation but anxious not knowing what mood they will be in a what I might have unknowingly done wrong.

We all have a dream of what we want our future to be. Now that you have acknowledged the narcissist in your life, why do you want this change? Why do you want to heal? Your "why" is important, and remembering your "why" will help move you forward. You might think about what you've been through. Think about what you picture your best future to be without this person's influence. What do you dream of doing that you are currently not able to do? What do you want to be? How do you want to feel?

I want to feel accepted for being me, with all my imperfections and flaws I want marriage, security and above all trust.

Taking Inventory of Abuse

The first step toward recovery is acknowledgment. It's time to take honest stock of how you have been harmed. How specifically has the narcissist victimized you?

Put a check mark next to the types of abuse that have applied to you in this relationship.

Psychological/Emotional

- ☐ Name-calling
- ☐ Yelling
- ☐ Controlling what you can or cannot do
- ☑ Withholding information
- ☐ Denying access to money or other resources
- ☐ Stalking
- ☐ Convincing you that you are crazy
- ☐ Threatening to die by suicide if you leave
- ☐ Threatening to kill loved ones or pets
- ☐ Destroying something important to you
- ☐ Blaming you for their abusive behavior

Physical Threats of Violence

- ☐ Physical assault
- ☐ Physical restraint
- ☐ Preventing you from eating or sleeping
- ☑ Sexual assault

Financial

- ☐ Not allowing you to go to work or school
- ☐ Controlling money
- ☐ Stealing money or possessions
- ☐ Creating a forced dependency

Digital

- ☐ Monitoring emails and texts
- ☒ Posting hurtful information or pictures on social media
- ☐ Sending threatening texts or emails

No matter how few or many items you checked off, it's too many. You deserve so much better, and this book will help you get there.

Also, please take pride in what you accomplish here. This is not easy work, and you have shown bravery just by reading and responding. Take breaks when this work feels heavy. There is no rush.

What are the indicators that this person is a narcissist? When did you first realize the situation you were in? Whom did you talk to about it? How long have you been trying to make sense of your situation? What do you keep thinking you should do about it but are afraid to do?

_____

_____

_____

_____

_____

_____

_____

_____

_____

_____

_____

_____

_____

_____

_____

_____

Healthy Responses to Anger

It's a good sign if you are feeling anger. It indicates that you are taking in the truth of what's going on. Holding on to some anger is good. It helps you stand up for your rights. But it's also important to find healthy ways to channel anger and keep it at bay. Here are some ideas:

→ **Step away and take some deep breaths.**

→ **Let go of the incident by focusing on things you value about yourself.**

→ **Replace negative thoughts. Instead of thinking this is a horrible thing that happened, replace it with *This will pass*.**

→ **Relax. Consider what is relaxing to you and turn to it.**

→ **Move your body. Burn off tension and stress that can fuel anger.**

You can manage your angry feelings by making changes to how you respond.

Empathy requires the ability to feel what it is like for the other person. Narcissists who are on the severe end of the narcissistic spectrum are incapable of empathy. Sadly, there is very little to no hope that an extreme narcissist has the interest or desire to change. Therefore, expecting this person to be part of your healing will only cause you disappointment. Healing and growing is your thing. Write about any disappointments or frustrations you might have about needing to be the one to do this work.

_____

_____

_____

_____

_____

_____

_____

_____

_____

_____

_____

_____

_____

_____

_____

_____

Write the story about a difficult situation that you had with the narcissist that you handled in a positive way. The story should have a beginning, a middle, and an end. How does this story affect how you think about yourself? What helped you deal with the situation? What were you most proud of?

_____

_____

_____

_____

_____

_____

_____

_____

_____

_____

_____

_____

_____

_____

_____

_____

_____

_____

_____

Self-Acceptance Meditation

You have been on an emotional roller coaster. Narcissists have a way of dumping their own buried feelings of insignificance and defectiveness on others. These actions are barriers to intimacy. You might not know what it feels like to be loved and accepted for who you really are.

Acceptance is the beginning. Try this meditation:

1. **Take a full breath through your nose and exhale through your mouth. Relax into the support of gravity.**

2. **As you inhale again, say to yourself,** *I am not a victim.*

3. **As you exhale, say to yourself,** *I have been victimized.*

4. **Do this breathing pattern 10 times.**

5. **Now, stand up and take a walk around your space with your head held high, shoulders back, chest out, and eyes open. Feel a new sense of yourself.**

6. **Repeat this exercise often.**

You are a victim when you are used by someone to feed their unquenchable thirst for validation. With this perspective on the role you've been in, you shift into an empowered stance. You are someone who has endured abuse, and you are finding ways to feed and bolster yourself rather than being in the position of helplessness.

Narcissists gravitate toward people who can "see" and mirror them because of their own unmet emotional and developmental needs for validation. Are you agreeable and easygoing? Do you put the needs of others before your needs? Is it difficult to ask for what you need? If you are nodding your head yes, you are vulnerable to a narcissist's ability to blindside you with a false sense of security and intimacy. Explore in writing how your generous personality might cause you to easily get stuck in a toxic relationship dynamic.

_____

_____

_____

_____

_____

_____

_____

_____

_____

_____

_____

_____

_____

_____

_____

_____

Accepting Your Flaws

Narcissists were dehumanized by someone who was supposed to care for them, and tend to continue this pattern into their adulthood. Because they can't stand their own inadequacies, they can't tolerate inadequacy in others and project their shame and insecurity onto those around them. Chances are the narcissist in your life has caused you to feel like having flaws and being human aren't allowed. Since this section is about self-acceptance, take some time to reflect on your own flaws. What are your insecurities? What qualities or traits do you feel you aren't "allowed" to have? Make a list.

_____

_____

_____

_____

_____

_____

_____

_____

_____

Now, go over these and think about how each one of these traits makes you human. Think about where each trait came from and how it reflects some part of your story—just like a knot on a tree's trunk tells some part of its journey from sapling to towering giant. You are a growing, living being. By recognizing and accepting your own flaws, you take an important step toward healing and becoming more whole.

Learning to manage stress and uncomfortable feelings is an ongoing process. Stress-management skills will help you sleep, release muscle tension, manage weight, get along with others better, and get sick less often. Reflect and list some unhealthy ways you may handle stress. Then list one healthy stress-management tool you want to try. It could be meditation, walking, breathing, yoga, a hobby, etc. Write out a plan for how and when you will practice managing stress in a healthy way.

_____

_____

_____

_____

_____

_____

_____

_____

_____

_____

_____

_____

_____

_____

_____

Almost everything will work
again if you unplug it for a few
minutes, including you.

—Anne Lamott

When you are in a constant state of threat, your focus naturally zeroes in on defending yourself. If your language has the tone of blame and name-calling, you are in victim mode. When you can pause and manage your emotions, you become a non-reactive, steady person who is in control of their life. Think about a situation where you felt defensive and write down how you reacted or protected yourself. Then write the situation out again, but this time make up a different ending, in which you respond in a way that is empowering.

_____

_____

_____

_____

_____

_____

_____

_____

_____

_____

_____

_____

_____

_____

_____

_____

_____

_____

List all the ways you have tried to fix or change yourself to make the narcissist in your life happy. You may have gone to therapy to figure out what was wrong with you. You might have changed your physical appearance or cut people out of your life. These are examples of how you may have internalized the abuser's messages. By making an inventory of what you have done to shape yourself to fit in or minimize conflict will help you become more aware and begin to make choices by listening to yourself.

List all the ways you have tried to fix or change the narcissist in your life. You might have tried to teach them how to listen and not interrupt, take responsibility and apologize, or participate in self-development workshops. Write about what you continue to want to change about them and how trying makes you feel.

_____

_____

_____

_____

_____

_____

_____

_____

_____

_____

_____

_____

_____

_____

_____

_____

_____

Confronting a person who has caused you pain can be incredibly empowering. In a situation with a narcissist, it isn't wise to do because of the likelihood of them turning on you and causing more destruction. There is a way to express your feelings that is safe and healthy. Write a letter that won't be sent. In this letter, imagine that you can say exactly how you were hurt. Say how angry you are and don't hold back. If you need more room, feel free to write in a notebook or journal.

Gaslighting is a phenomenon in which one person attempts to avoid taking responsibility for their behavior by attacking the other person's account of what they have been doing wrong. The one doing the gaslighting is rarely conscious of it. This doesn't make the behavior any less controlling or confusing, though.

Gaslighting might sound like "You're overreacting again," or "I have no idea what you're talking about," or "It's your fault that I am reacting this way, because you know how I feel about this and you did it anyway." It translates into "Everything wrong with this relationship is your fault and you need to tolerate my abuse." Does this sound familiar? How has this affected you?

_____

_____

_____

_____

_____

_____

_____

_____

_____

_____

_____

_____

_____

Acknowledging the abuse by someone who was supposed to love you will force the question of why you try to get love from an unloving person. In her book *Unloved Again*, Elan Golomb writes, "A person raised by a bully marries a bully and remains consistently unhappy." What were your parents/caregivers like? Were you raised by a narcissist? Do you see a pattern in choosing to love people that's propelled by a need to reexperience early-life abuse? Are you somehow choosing to be unloved? Why do you think you try to be loved by a person who is incapable of loving you?

_____

_____

_____

_____

_____

_____

_____

_____

_____

_____

_____

_____

_____

_____

_____

I can do hard things.

Be patient with yourself.
Self-growth is tender;
it's holy ground. There's no
greater investment.

—*Stephen Covey*

Practice Self-Love and Self-Compassion

The emotional distress of dealing with a narcissist can leave you exhausted, overwhelmed, ashamed, and doubting yourself. Self-compassion and self-love are essential next steps on the road to recovery. Being compassionate with yourself rather than judgmental will allow space for understanding of and tenderness for the pain of your past and present.

Mindfulness is an important component in practicing self-compassion. According to Jon Kabat-Zinn, founder of mindfulness-based stress reduction (MBSR), mindfulness is "the awareness that arises from paying attention, on purpose, in the present moment and nonjudgmentally." Mindfulness provides a way to let go of your belief of how things should be and open up to the reality of what is. In this way you can simply be with any suffering with courage and presence. This section provides you with tools that will help you love your whole self.

The three components of self-compassion are 1) becoming aware of the pain, 2) offering kind support and care for our pain, and 3) recognizing that we are not alone in our suffering—there are others experiencing the pain of narcissistic abuse. When we realize that we are a part of humanity, we feel less alone. Through kind words, offer yourself some tender compassion and finish by sending out a wish for healing to everyone and everything else that suffers.

_____

_____

_____

_____

_____

_____

_____

_____

_____

_____

_____

_____

_____

_____

_____

Self-compassion and self-love may feel awkward, as you have been so accustomed to focusing on the narcissist in your life. By focusing on yourself, you might reveal resistance in the form of guilt. Take a couple of slow breaths and tune in to your thoughts and sensations. Offer yourself some understanding by acknowledging *I hear and see you*. Write down that statement and then write about any guilt or resistance you may have to focusing on yourself.

Shift Your Resistance

Read the resistant thought in the left column and rate how true it seems (from 1 being not true to 5 being very true). Then read the realistic thought in the right column three times, slowly taking a breath as you read. Rate how true the second statement feels.

RESISTANT THOUGHT	RATE 1-5	REALISTIC THOUGHT	RATE 1-5
Having self-compassion and self-love is selfish.	4	I am not effective at helping others unless I have taken good care of myself.	5
Being kind to myself makes me weak. I need to be tough to be powerful.	3	The ability to listen to and be with myself when I am vulnerable is what gives me strength. Being tough is exhausting.	4

RESISTANT THOUGHT	RATE 1-5	REALISTIC THOUGHT	RATE 1-5
It's too late to learn something new. I am set in my ways.	2	People can change and grow. Science shows that our minds reshape when we have intention.	5
It's silly to imagine giving myself compassion.		By listening to my inner longings, I am honoring my true self.	

Part of having compassion for yourself means allowing yourself to experience your feelings—positive or negative. It's natural to avoid or run from uncomfortable feelings. Common ways to avoid or escape are alcohol and/or drugs, sex, food, overexercise, shopping, surfing the internet, gambling, etc. How do you attempt to escape painful feelings of anxiety, anger, or sadness?

_____

_____

_____

_____

_____

_____

_____

_____

_____

_____

_____

_____

_____

_____

_____

_____

What exactly are you feeling right now? The field of positive psychology tells us that there are about 34,000 different feelings. The primary feelings that are the foundation for all the others are fear, disgust, joy, acceptance, sadness, surprise, and anticipation. Practicing mindfulness helps you identify your feelings. Mindfulness means being with the present moment. Close your eyes, take a couple of breaths, and become mindful of what you feel. It could be a physical sensation or an emotion. Please open your eyes and write it down.

_____

_____

_____

_____

_____

_____

_____

_____

_____

_____

_____

_____

_____

_____

Tuning In to Sensations

1. Set a timer for five minutes.

2. Sit comfortably in a quiet place, close your eyes, and pay attention to what it feels like to be in your body. Be with the physical sensations as they come and go without choosing to stay with any particular one. Perhaps you'll feel the weight of your body in the chair and how your feet are positioned. Notice the temperature difference where there is clothing covering skin. If the sensation is pleasant, let it go. If the sensation is unpleasant, let it go.

3. Notice these sensations as if you were compassionately watching over a beloved sleeping baby, wondering what they are feeling. All you need to do is notice one sensation after another. Take your time.

4. When your timer goes off, open your eyes.

Pay attention to how you might be judging your own feelings. You could be realizing a pattern from when you were little and thinking, *You shouldn't feel that way!* or *Don't cry—it makes you weak.* What messages did you receive about feelings growing up? How were your feelings responded to by the narcissist in your life?

_____

_____

_____

_____

_____

_____

_____

_____

_____

_____

_____

_____

_____

_____

_____

_____

_____

The thought of being kind to yourself might feel impossible. Are you finding your-self predominantly feeling angry, fidgety, and frustrated? Are you mad at yourself for being overly sensitive or for being told you should be more compassionate with yourself? Holding on to anger can be a way to cover up the painful longing to feel connected. How does holding on to self-directed anger keep you from having a tender, soft acceptance of who you are? What are you afraid will happen if you let go of anger and feel your longing to be connected? Write your feelings here.

_____

_____

_____

_____

_____

_____

_____

_____

_____

_____

_____

_____

_____

_____

_____

When you replay all the incidents that were less than great when your head hits the pillow at the end of the day, you fall asleep with the message "You have failed." When you flip this and replay the positive moments in the day, you transform beyond being stuck in negative emotional loops. Write three things that happened today that you feel good about.

_____

_____

_____

_____

_____

_____

_____

_____

_____

_____

_____

_____

_____

_____

Messages of Goodness

Bring to mind a familiar presence that's easy to love. It could be a person you know, a loving grandparent, a divine being, or an animal. Imagine looking into their eyes as they look back with love. Imagine the natural tenderness that's there. Express with your eyes their goodness, and then imagine them recognizing your goodness. Now take this out into the world and practice. Consciously look at someone you encounter directly in their eyes, while consciously sending them the thought that you recognize their goodness. (This doesn't need to be a long gaze; it can happen in a flash.) When you walk away, spend a moment to reflect on the experience.

Celebrate that you don't have to take in negativity from the narcissist. In the space below, write two affirming phrases that feel comforting and reassuring. If you need ideas, think of an appropriate source, such as what a good parent would say to a young child who had just been upset by something, what a respected leader would tell their worker to encourage them, or what a good friend or partner would say in hard times. Explain why these particular messages feel so reassuring to you.

Just keep coming home to yourself. You are the one you've been waiting for.

—*Byron Katie*

Do you have "should-itis"? Do you often find yourself arguing with yourself over what you *want* to do versus what you feel like you *should* do? Sometimes self-compassion means going inside yourself and asking yourself what is really important right now. What internal or external voice is driving your decisions? Do you often feel that you need to do more to feel good enough? Write about what it would be like to accept the feeling that you are good enough just as you are.

_____

_____

_____

_____

_____

_____

_____

_____

_____

_____

_____

_____

_____

_____

_____

_____

_____

The voice of a shaming parent, abusive romantic partner, or boss has a way of taking residence in your head and becoming your inner critic. But there is also a wise adult-self residing in you and holding this journal. Write a letter from your wise adult-self to your inner critic. Thank it for its part in helping you survive a time where you had to remain small to keep the peace, but you realize this bossy, damaging part of yourself has been working overtime and is going into retirement. Please write your letter: Dear inner critic . . .

TV and social media bombard us with messages that tell us what we should look like, what we should do, what medicines we should be taking, and how many "likes" we need to be worthy. As a result, we mask up to fit in, concealing who we are. Hiding beneath a persona also happens in a narcissistic relationship, because we conform to who they need us to be. How do you hide? What do you hide? How can you align more with your real self?

_____

_____

_____

_____

_____

_____

_____

_____

_____

_____

_____

_____

_____

_____

_____

Giving yourself the compassion you long for may bring up painful memories of when compassion wasn't there. This is part of moving forward. How do you feel when you think about moments from the past when you needed compassion? Anger can be part of grief. Allow yourself to be messy as you write about grief.

_____

_____

_____

_____

_____

_____

_____

_____

_____

_____

_____

_____

_____

_____

_____

_____

Think about reframing your experience. You are not a victim. You were victimized. How can you transform your situation into something good? When you speak about yourself saying *yes, BUT*, you reinforce being a powerless victim. When you say *yes, AND*, you are reframing your experience into something positive that came out of difficulty. Write a paragraph stating what happened and how you are reframing the experience into something good.

_____

_____

_____

_____

_____

_____

_____

_____

_____

_____

_____

_____

_____

_____

_____

_____

_____

Creating Heart Space

Part of self-compassion and self-love is protecting a younger version of yourself—your inner child, who has been with you your whole life. This inner child has experienced every moment of fear, abuse, and abandonment that you have. Imagine nurturing this younger version of yourself by creating a safe place in your heart where your inner child and your present self are always welcome. By doing this, you give your inner child the message that there is now a nurturing, safe place, protected by a warm and powerful adult who refuses to engage in self-hatred and self-abandonment.

With any art supplies you have available, draw an image of your inner child safely held in your heart.

Listening to my spirit and being kind to myself puts me on my path.

The Universe buries strange jewels
deep within us all, and then stands
back to see if we can find them.

—*Elizabeth Gilbert*

Reclaim Your True Self

A narcissist may go to extraordinary lengths to avoid encountering their own overwhelming feelings of shame and often tries to control, manipulate, or bully the people around them. This dynamic doesn't leave much room for you to express your authentic thoughts and feelings. The resulting feelings of disconnectedness from who we are feel painful and cause suffering. In this section, you will unearth the buried and lost parts of yourself as you continue to acknowledge your inner child, your wise adult self, and your inner critic. Now you can begin to rebuild your connection and confidence in your authentic self. Some of the key ways to achieve this include engaging in positive self-talk and overcoming negative thinking, as well as being non-judgmental and letting go of self-criticism. Instead, you can think about your values, strengths, commitments, and everything else you have to offer the world and yourself.

You have been wronged and are looking at how you made choices to go along with it. You learned to silence your needs even though your gut told you not to. Imagining your ideal day gives a voice to that part of you that has been longing for attention. Using a first-person perspective, write down what happens on your ideal day. Where and how do you wake up? What do you do? How do you dress? Who is included in your day? How do you wind down at the end of the day? Be specific and descriptive, using your senses and recognizing what is most important to you. When you finish, identify one thing you can do now that will bring you closer to your ideal day.

\

\

\

\

\

\

\

\

\

\

\

\

\

\

\

\

\

In what ways have you silenced yourself in your relationship with a narcissist? How much do other people's opinions and judgments matter to you? Are lost parts showing up now, such as gender identity, creativity, spirituality, appearance, friends, family, hobbies, and activities? Let them show up here on this page.

_____

_____

_____

_____

_____

_____

_____

_____

_____

_____

_____

_____

_____

_____

_____

_____

_____

_____

It's easy for the inner critic to chime in when we try to grow and change. Critical thoughts can function as a defense, keeping us from experiencing the discomfort of the unknown. By noticing the critical thoughts, you can choose to let them pass through and make space for more encouraging thoughts. What is your inner critic saying about the changes you are making? What encouraging thoughts want to move into their place?

_____

_____

_____

_____

_____

_____

_____

_____

_____

_____

_____

_____

_____

_____

Reframing Beliefs

Self-encouragement is an excellent way to replace self-criticism and negative beliefs. It's also a way to shift out of the victim trap. When you focus on criticizing the lying, cheating, selfishness, and ridicule of the narcissist in your life, you tell yourself that you are powerless. That's not who you are. You are a survivor. It's time to move out of the victim's seat and into the seat of healing and rediscovering yourself. You are learning to be empowered. Whenever you catch yourself being critical of yourself or someone else, reframe the thought into an encouraging statement; use this strategy to shift from the negative to the positive.

OLD NEGATIVE BELIEF AND HOW IT FORMED	WHAT HAPPENS IF I HOLD ON TO THIS BELIEF	REFRAME TO A NEW BELIEF
Example: I'm not capable; reinforced by coworker	*Example: I won't push myself to new opportunities*	*Example: I dictate my own success—not another person.*

What Is Your Posture Saying?

We slouch, collapse, and limit body language when we feel powerless. When others observe us doing those things, they see us as powerless and afraid. First, assume a slouched posture (shoulders caved in and head drooping down) and hold the shape for one minute. What happens for you? Next, stand upright (back straight, eyes forward, and shoulders back) and hold this shape for one minute. How does this feel?

SLOUCHED	
How does it feel to stand like this?	
How different is it from how you are used to standing?	
What are your negative beliefs in this posture?	
What are your positive beliefs in this posture?	

UPRIGHT	
How does it feel to stand like this?	
How different is it from how you are used to standing?	
What are your negative beliefs in this posture?	
What are your positive beliefs in this posture?	

A narcissist's manipulations can quash your ability to be the judge of who you are. When you rely on negative external sources to give you worth, your self-esteem declines. Instead, surround yourself with a positive circle of friends and family who can help remind you how good you are and the kind of people you deserve to be around. Who are the people in your life that offer you positive support? Make a list here.

_____

_____

_____

_____

_____

_____

_____

_____

_____

_____

_____

_____

_____

_____

_____

_____

_____

What if, from now on, you become the author of the new story of your life? For this, you don't need an editor. Don't let anyone else hold the pen. Write a paragraph about the burdens of your narcissistic relationship. Follow with a paragraph about where you are right now. Finally, write a paragraph about how you will transition experiences of pain into power for yourself.

I'm discovering joy as
I become more of
who I am.

Write the story of what your future might look like if you gave up on yourself. Then, in writing, declare a new standard of who you want to be in the world. What do you have to live for, to rise to? Include your reality as well as your dreams.

_____

_____

_____

_____

_____

_____

_____

_____

_____

_____

_____

_____

_____

_____

_____

_____

_____

To say that I'm healed implies
that there's an end point . . .
Healing is something that we'll all
continually do for the rest of our lives.

—*Suleika Jaouad*

Three People and Three Strengths

Identify three people who know you well and whose opinion you trust. Reach out to them via email, text, or regular mail. Let them know you are working on changing some things in your life and that it would be helpful if they participated in a short survey. Ask them to respond to the following prompt:

What three strengths do you attribute to me? Please answer honestly. Thank you for taking the time to participate. I chose to ask you because I value your opinion.

The people who are close to you will likely be happy to offer their thoughts, especially if they know you're taking steps to improve your life. (You can practice silencing your inner critic that might be telling you otherwise, right now!)

Please keep track of how they respond here.

_____

_____

_____

_____

_____

_____

_____

_____

_____

_____

_____

Being in a relationship with a narcissist extinguishes hope. Let your imagination take you on a mini-vacation away from hopelessness, a land where dreams are allowed. In this land, you meet a genie in a bottle. Guess what? You are granted three wishes! What would you wish for? Write them down.

_____

_____

_____

_____

_____

_____

_____

_____

_____

_____

_____

_____

_____

_____

_____

Emotional well-being is not possible without physical well-being. Some general areas of health to attend to include a yearly physical exam, nutritious diet, hydration, exercise, dental health, sleep; they also include awareness of addiction and dependencies—such as overeating, smoking, drugs, and alcohol—and the need to get help with them (see Resources, page 134). Explore in writing where you are in regard to taking care of your physical health.

_____

_____

_____

_____

_____

_____

_____

_____

_____

_____

_____

_____

_____

_____

_____

_____

You can free yourself from setting aside your needs and desires to get along with your narcissist. It's time to experience what pleases *you*. What sort of things do you wish for? What are your fantasies of doing things differently? How do you turn yourself on and experience joy? How do you turn yourself off and slink away from life? What are you afraid of doing because you fear failing?

_____

_____

_____

_____

_____

_____

_____

_____

_____

_____

_____

_____

_____

_____

We all have character strengths that support us throughout our lives. What are your strengths? How have they helped you get through some tough circumstances?

_____

_____

_____

_____

_____

_____

_____

_____

_____

_____

_____

_____

_____

_____

_____

_____

_____

Imagine 10 years from now your friends and family gather to celebrate you in some way. What would you like them to say about you in the speeches they give? Pick five of these people and write what you would ideally want them to say (even if you haven't yet done what they would say).

_____

_____

_____

_____

_____

_____

_____

_____

_____

_____

_____

_____

_____

_____

_____

_____

_____

_____

When you are in a relationship with a narcissist, thinking about the future can be stressful. It's easy to get anxious anticipating negative events. Think about an event in your future that causes stress when you think about it? Name the event and write a positive affirmation related specifically to it.

_____

_____

_____

_____

_____

_____

_____

_____

_____

_____

_____

_____

_____

_____

_____

_____

_____

What do you want your life to stand for? What are commitments that align with your values? What's most meaningful to you? Write about each of the following areas of your life: health, wealth, relationships, work, and spirituality.

_____

_____

_____

_____

_____

_____

_____

_____

_____

_____

_____

_____

_____

_____

_____

_____

_____

_____

Self-Fulfilling Vision Board

Find pictures representing the feelings, experiences, and things you want in your life. These can include photographs, magazines, images from the internet, etc. Also include words, affirmations, quotations, and thoughts that inspire you and make you feel good.

You'll need:

→ **Piece of cardboard or poster board**

→ **Pictures and words**

→ **Paper and marker or pen**

→ **Scissors**

→ **Glue**

Create a collage incorporating the feel-good images and words. Display it where you will see it regularly. Spend a minute or two every day imagining that it is all already true. You can take a photo of your vision board and use it as your wallpaper on your phone. From this collage, you will find yourself automatically making decisions that move you closer to your vision.

Each time we don't honor our own boundaries, and each time others don't honor who we are, an old wound is deepened.

—*Nancy Van Dyken*

Clear Boundaries Will Help You Heal

While much of healing and recovery happens internally, it's also important to set boundaries for your external environment. Boundaries create separateness between yourself and someone else, making your life your own and making sure your rights are honored. How can you protect yourself from now on? How can you create a safe, supportive, and nurturing environment for yourself? How can you create space between yourself and the narcissist? Boundaries can apply to physical, mental, emotional, and social needs. You will know you are on a good path of recovery when you realize you are your own unshakable source of compassion and protection. In this section, you have an opportunity to practice being your own best advocate. You will increase your self-awareness, identify boundary violations from childhood, and consider the conditions of boundaries in your current relationships. Above all, you will get closer to prioritizing your needs.

When you are feeling bullied or intimidated by a narcissist, it isn't easy to set limits and boundaries because they manipulate you to do it their way. Describe a recent situation where you felt disrespected or used. What was the situation? As you replay this memory, pay attention to the sensations in your body. Is there an impulse to pull back, withdraw, freeze? How did you handle it? How might you do it differently in the future? If this prompt causes an intense response of anxiety or panic, remind yourself that in this moment, you are safe. Take a slow, deep breath. You can come back to this prompt another time.

Physical Boundary Experience

1. Find a bunch of pillows or other objects and arrange them in a big circle.

2. Sit quietly in your circle. Take several conscious breaths as you sense the space around you, both inside and outside the circle.

3. If any place in the circle you created feels vulnerable or unprotected, add more objects until you feel a sense of security. Make sure the circle is the right distance from you and that the shape around you feels right—this is your space.

4. Please spend a few minutes here experiencing what it's like to have your own space.

Is there a type of interaction with the narcissist you can stop? Narcissists will want to hang around trying to get attention. Can you implement a no-contact boundary? This means disconnecting both physically and emotionally, such as by blocking social media on your phone and avoiding sentimental journeys of rereading texts and looking at pictures from the past. If you are co-parenting with a narcissist, is there a way to have limited direct contact? How and what sort of contact is best for you?

_____

_____

_____

_____

_____

_____

_____

_____

_____

_____

_____

_____

_____

_____

_____

What things would you like to say no to? Knowing what you no longer wish to tolerate will help you define how to protect yourself with good boundaries. You might think about a situation from the past where you wanted to say no but found yourself going along with it to avoid conflict. If you had the strength now, what would you say no to?

_____

_____

_____

_____

_____

_____

_____

_____

_____

_____

_____

_____

_____

_____

_____

_____

_____

_____

What's Beneath Your Mask?

By exploring the differences between your internal self and how you present yourself externally, you will reveal how you protect yourself. This persona may or may not be serving you in knowing what boundaries you need.

YOU'LL NEED:

Magazines   **Tape or glue**

Scissors   **Paper grocery bag**

1. Reflect on how you present yourself externally.

2. Cut out pictures and words that represent how you present yourself externally. Tape or glue them to the outside of the bag.

3. Reflect on your internal self.

4. Cut out pictures and words that represent your inner self. Put these cutouts inside the bag.

5. When you have finished, take time to compare the words and pictures inside and outside the bag. Have you represented two different people, or are you describing a harmonious, congruent self? Discuss what you have revealed with a friend.

Who are you without the persona you adopted in your relationship with a narcissist? Describe a real-life situation with the narcissist where you know you wear a "mask." Then write about the same situation as if you are grounded and present with your true self. What would be different showing up as your authentic self?

_____

_____

_____

_____

_____

_____

_____

_____

_____

_____

_____

_____

_____

_____

_____

_____

_____

_____

Reinforcing Boundaries

Reflect on your current situation, then circle the types of boundaries you need to be aware of and strengthen. For circled areas, note why you feel you need to strengthen this area.

BOUNDARY		WHY I NEED TO STRENGTHEN THIS AREA:
Physical	Physical boundary violations happen when someone touches you when you don't want them to or when your space is invaded.	
Intellectual	Intellectual boundary violations happen when someone takes responsibility for your ideas/work or dismisses or belittles your thoughts and ideas.	
Emotional	Emotional boundary violations happen when there aren't limitations on what others share and who they share it with regarding your personal information.	

BOUNDARY		WHY I NEED TO STRENGTHEN THIS AREA:
Sexual	Sexual boundary violations happen when there are unwanted sexual comments or contact, or pressure to engage in sexual acts.	
Material	Material violations happen when someone steals or damages your possessions, or pressures you to give or lend them.	
Time	Time boundary violations happen when you give too much of your time to something at the expense of your well-being, or someone demands too much of your time.	
Digital	Digital boundary violations happen when someone snoops or copies digital information or uses the internet to bully, coerce, or emotionally shame.	

With hindsight, we can visualize how we could have protected ourselves against the different kinds of boundary violations discussed in the previous exercise. If you could magically go back in time and change something about an interaction you had, either in relation to the previous exercise or something that happened today, what would it be? What sort of boundary would fit in this situation?

_____

_____

_____

_____

_____

_____

_____

_____

_____

_____

_____

_____

_____

_____

Reflect on the following statement: *My well-being is determined by what others think about me.*

Does this statement resonate with you? What do you do to please others to feel better about yourself? Include your thoughts about how this behavior gives others power over your self-esteem. What is one thing you could do for yourself to feel more relaxed about just being who you are?

_____

_____

_____

_____

_____

_____

_____

_____

_____

_____

_____

_____

_____

_____

_____

"Yes" and "no" answers are effective in setting boundaries. This is easily done when you are clear about your preferences. When you're caught off guard or perhaps your people-pleaser self is telling you to feel guilty if you say no, it's not so easy. You can set a boundary by giving yourself time to think. Imagine a friend is asking you for an unexpected favor, and you're not clear on your "yes" or "no." Write down how you will respond, letting your friend know that you need time to think about it.

_____

_____

_____

_____

_____

_____

_____

_____

_____

_____

_____

_____

_____

_____

A person's success in life can usually be measured by the number of uncomfortable conversations he or she is willing to have.

—*Tim Ferriss*

Being kind doesn't mean that you can't stand up for yourself. Standing up for yourself in the form of setting boundaries is a way of expressing your needs. Boundaries also determine if you receive respect from others. Can you refuse to accept abuse? What emotions come up when you think about standing up for yourself?

_____

_____

_____

_____

_____

_____

_____

_____

_____

_____

_____

_____

_____

_____

_____

_____

Compassionate Listening

The next time someone shares something distressing with you, listen with your whole body, allowing sensations to emerge as you pay attention with your eyes and ears. Send out loving presence in the form of imaginary light beaming from your heart. Notice your own reactions of wanting to interrupt, becoming engulfed by what you hear, or feeling the urge to fix their problem with advice. When your attention wanders off, breathe in compassion for yourself as you consciously inhale, and breathe out compassion for the speaker as you exhale. This brings you back to a loving connection without losing yourself. Compassionate listening will help you be with someone sharing a painful situation in their life without taking on their emotional pain.

Personal boundaries are the limits and rules created within a relationship. With **healthy boundaries**, you can say no or yes when it's comfortable. When a person always keeps others at a distance, they have **rigid boundaries**. When a person gets too involved with others, they have **porous boundaries**. Think about a situation from your past that may have created either porous or rigid boundaries. What was going on that affected your boundaries in this way? In hindsight, how might you manage this situation differently?

_____

_____

_____

_____

_____

_____

_____

_____

_____

_____

_____

_____

_____

_____

_____

_____

Think of a time when you lost yourself in an interaction with someone else, meaning you wanted to say no but didn't, or you felt pressured to do something against your values. Write the story of this situation, describing the ways you denied yourself and how that felt. See yourself after the situation had passed. Were you aware of your boundaries at that time?

_____

_____

_____

_____

_____

_____

_____

_____

_____

_____

_____

_____

_____

_____

_____

_____

_____

Think about a time that you stayed connected to your true self. Write the story of the situation, describing the ways you felt clear and connected to yourself. How did that feel? See yourself after the situation had passed. Were you aware of your boundaries at that time? Did you have a clear sense of yourself? How did you reinforce your boundaries?

Who was important and influential to you as a child? Did you experience a boundary violation such as inappropriate touch or abandonment, or a fuzzy boundary such as neglect of your emotional needs or an expectation for you to take on adult caretaking responsibilities? These events could have happened within your family, school, club, team, or religious organization. What was wrong and what was confusing about this experience? (If this prompt brings up memories resulting in panic-like anxiety, consider reaching out to a professional who can help you work through childhood trauma. See page 134 for resources.)

_____

_____

_____

_____

_____

_____

_____

_____

_____

_____

_____

_____

_____

How do you relate to people who depend on you, such as children, clients, or more junior colleagues at work? Are you behaving as a peer rather than a mentor in any of these relationships? How do you relate to people who provide care or supervision to you, such as a supervisor, doctor, or therapist? Do you want them to be a friend? Write about some moments in which the roles became blurred and difficult to navigate, and identify a plan for cleaning up these relationship boundaries going forward.

Each time I honor my boundaries, I feel more confident about expressing my needs.

Very few highly resilient individuals go it alone and neither should you.

—*Dennis Charney*

SECTION 5

Open Yourself Up to Healthy Relationships

In this section, you will learn the building blocks of a healthy relationship. When someone is drawn to a narcissist, it is often because of an ingrained knowledge of how to navigate within that sort of relationship. It's possible that you learned this from narcissistic parents. As an adult, you can find yourself in the midst of narcissists over and over; however, you can also learn from your past and come to recognize problematic patterns. In this section, you'll acquire tools to let go of people-pleasing and nurture the great relationships you already have.

Your community is your teacher and a vital part of how you experience the world. Surrounding yourself with people who lift you up instead of pulling you down takes hard work, because you are practicing new ways of relating. It's time to acknowledge the healthy people already in your life and explore ways to add to your circle.

It's likely that your self-esteem has sustained some damage by the narcissist and you're feeling insecure. Positive psychology teaches that how other people interact with you can have a significant effect on your self-esteem. Think about your circle of people, and answer these questions, focusing on how their strengths bolster your esteem: Who is the most positive and optimistic person in your circle? Who is the most humorous and playful? Who treats others fairly? Who is the most loving? Who is the most forgiving? Who seems balanced and able to self-regulate?

_____

_____

_____

_____

_____

_____

_____

_____

_____

_____

_____

_____

_____

_____

_____

_____

Seeds of New Relationships

Make an audio or video recording of yourself reciting the following text or something like it. Listen to it regularly throughout your healing journey.

In this moment, I am safe, and it's all right to be calm. I am on relaxation and repair time.

My heart is seeking positive relationships. In my mind, I see a garden planted with seeds of wonderful partnerships, friendships, or work relationships. I shower these seeds with love as warm rain and sun enrich the soil of my heart's wishes. I deserve to have people who I am inspired to love and be around. I deserve a community that makes me happy to belong. In my mind, I open my heart wide to bring in the sun and the rain. I welcome these promising new blooms of relationship. I delight in visualizing my prospering garden of relationships and the joy they will bring.

Are you a people pleaser? If so, you might get overinvolved in other people's problems, making you attractive to a narcissist. Do you have the habit of overlooking people's negative behaviors? If so, the charismatic charm of a narcissist can sweep you off your feet. How did you get caught up by a narcissist in the past? If you're in a new relationship, how can you take time alone and/or with a trusted confidant to figure out what to do (such as test boundaries, talk it through with the new person, or cut loose) before it's too late?

_____

_____

_____

_____

_____

_____

_____

_____

_____

_____

_____

_____

_____

_____

_____

_____

_____

If you have a pattern of falling in love quickly and dramatically, the feeling of being special to someone who is flattering you may blind you to red-flag warnings. Before you fall into this trap, turning inward to heal the parts of yourself that may need it will help you build self-esteem, make better choices, and ultimately resist the pull of narcissistic seduction. Write a vow to yourself to stay committed to your healing path.

_____

_____

_____

_____

_____

_____

_____

_____

_____

_____

_____

_____

_____

What interests have you left behind that you might want to get involved with again? Where do you feel a connection? What ideas have you kept on the back burner? Do you have a hobby that got dropped when life got stressful? Write about what lights you up. What have you been missing? Who's been missing you?

_____

_____

_____

_____

_____

_____

_____

_____

_____

_____

_____

_____

_____

_____

_____

_____

Who are your supporters, and how can you add to this list? Beyond friends and family, how about a fitness trainer, parenting coach, psychotherapist, spiritual counselor, business coach, massage therapist, hairstylist, nutritionist, professional organizer, writing group, or support group of any sorts. Make a list of who you have on board now. List new supporters you think you may benefit from, and make a plan to connect. You can add more as time goes on.

_____

_____

_____

_____

_____

_____

_____

_____

_____

_____

_____

_____

_____

_____

_____

_____

"I" statements in communication are a great way to take responsibility for your feelings. Using "I" statements when you are expressing a need will reduce the possibility of the other person getting defensive. "I" statements take the blame out of the equation.

I statement format: I feel _____ when you _____ because _____.

Let's try it out: Your friend is consistently late for appointments with you. You feel angry and need to let them know. Write how you can let your friend know how their lateness makes you feel, using the nonblaming "I" statement format.

_____

_____

_____

_____

_____

_____

_____

_____

_____

_____

_____

_____

_____

_____

Find a Support Group

Participating in a support group while forming healthy relationships can be the most powerful part of your healing. Whatever group you choose will bring like-minded people into your life. Support groups provide a place to be listened to, and you will realize that you are not alone with your challenges.

Do an online search for a group that fits your needs and schedule a time to attend. If possible, have a phone chat with someone from the group before the meeting to understand what to expect. There are support groups specifically for narcissistic abuse survivors, as well as other options in the Resources section (page 134). It can take several visits to a few groups to find the right one. Keep looking until you find a great fit for you.

We learn how to be in a "couple" relationship by how it was modeled to us. What did you internalize about love and relationships in your childhood? How did your parents relate to each other? How did they show affection to each other? How did they fight, and how did they make up? How have your adult romantic relationships mirrored the relationships you grew up with as a child?

_____

_____

_____

_____

_____

_____

_____

_____

_____

_____

_____

_____

_____

_____

_____

_____

If someone hurts you, say so. It's not your job to protect your partner, friend, or parent from knowing they've behaved badly. If they can't acknowledge your pain, they will continue to hurt you. You might be avoiding conflict by holding in your feelings. Suppressing your emotions affects your self-esteem. You gain respect from yourself and others when you speak up for yourself. Write about a situation in which you let someone think you were happy with them when you were not.

_____

_____

_____

_____

_____

_____

_____

_____

_____

_____

_____

_____

_____

_____

_____

_____

If you were romantically attached to a narcissist in the past and are now dating again, you might find a prospective partner who doesn't have narcissistic charisma to be uninteresting, boring, and mundane. Your radar may be more tuned in with someone who seems powerful or someone who is struggling somehow and needs the sort of help you can provide. What would it be like to be with someone reliable, steady, loyal, and devoted? Someone who adapts gracefully to stress or new situations? Someone who takes you as you are? Reflect and note your thoughts.

_____

_____

_____

_____

_____

_____

_____

_____

_____

_____

_____

_____

_____

_____

_____

When you feel secure with who you are within a relationship, you will feel more at ease and whole. A healthy relationship has a balance between alone time and together time. How are you with spending time with yourself? Do you feel compelled to attach to someone to avoid being alone? How do you spend your time when you are alone? Write about what it's like for you to be alone.

_____

_____

_____

_____

_____

_____

_____

_____

_____

_____

_____

_____

_____

_____

_____

_____

_____

_____

What qualities do you want in a partner? Spend some time thinking about how you would ideally resolve conflicts, how you would get along with each other's family, manage money, spend time together and alone, divide up chores, and share intimacy. What types of interactions do you long for?

_____

_____

_____

_____

_____

_____

_____

_____

_____

_____

_____

_____

_____

_____

_____

_____

_____

I allow only healthy and loving relationships in my life.

When you feel responsible for others' happiness, feelings of low self-worth follow, and you lose connection to what is valuable to you. Write about a recent incident in which you felt it was your responsibility to give more of yourself. After you write about this incident, look to see if you have feelings of anger, desire, self-judgment, impatience, or criticism. Conclude with how you want to show up differently.

Relational Flow of Energy

1. Sit quietly and bring to mind a close relationship in your life.

2. Bring in the energy of this person—make it real. How do you feel when you're with them? Imagine there is a cord that stretches from your heart to theirs. This cord carries information about this relationship. In what direction is the energy flowing? Do you feel like you're giving more and that energy is being pulled out of you? Or is it the energy flow reciprocal? What does the energy feel like coming from them? Does it feel restorative? Are there specific emotions and sensations?

3. Breathe as you do this, and let feelings like anger and grief come up. What do you want to do to make it better—perhaps change the direction of the energy, detach, make a larger or smaller boundary, or accept it for what it is? What needs to happen to help this relationship for you and the other person?

A healthy relationship includes things like playfulness, pleasure, and positive emotions. Write about two times you remember having the most fun. This event could be from childhood or recent memories. Describe the memory. How did this feel in your body? What emotions did you feel during this fun moment? What were your thoughts about yourself and others? Was this competitive play or play for no purpose other than fun? How could you incorporate playful activities both in your relationship and when you're alone?

_____

_____

_____

_____

_____

_____

_____

_____

_____

_____

_____

_____

_____

Connecting with the Earth

1. Sit comfortably in a chair.

2. Close your eyes or relax your gaze.

3. Feel your feet on the floor. Imagine being rooted into the ground, like a tree. Feel your roots being nourished and supported by all the earth has to offer.

4. Bring your attention to your body. Where do you feel your body in contact with the chair? Feel the effects of gravity as you scan any areas of your body where you might feel tension.

5. Next, bring your awareness to your breath. On a slow inhale, feel cool air filling your lungs, and on the exhale, feel the warm air leave and let go of any tension. Continue with three full inhales and exhales, focusing only on your breath and your body.

6. Before you finish, take a moment to sense your connection to the earth and yourself.

You are a person worthy of love.

—*Sharon Salzberg*

I will never have this version
of me again. Let me slow
down and be with her.

—*Rupi Kaur*

Put Your Self-Care First

Healing and recovering from narcissistic abuse is an ongoing journey. Your well-being depends on holding tight to your resolve of reclaiming your life. How can you lean into self-care every day to support your healing? Some constants:

→ **Take back your joy by putting your passions and dreams first.**

→ **Make time for yourself every day.**

→ **Speak kindly to yourself.**

→ **Reach out to your supportive community.**

Self-care allows you to feel more in control of your life in all aspects, including mental, physical, emotional, relational, and spiritual. Self-care involves clearly connecting to your own needs and wants daily. It's not something you wait to do until you're overwhelmed and exhausted. Self-care is rejuvenating to body and spirit, and as you make it a part of who you are, your self-care practice will evolve and grow with you.

Giving yourself some time to be mindfully engaged at the start of the day helps eliminate rushing and stress, starting you off on the right footing. What is your morning routine? Do you want to incorporate more time for self-care as you awaken? What is something you can do for the first 10 minutes of your day, before you plug in and start running, that connects you to your healing intention?

_____

_____

_____

_____

_____

_____

_____

_____

_____

_____

_____

_____

_____

_____

_____

_____

_____

What have you discovered about yourself throughout this journal? Which exercises were the most enlightening? How are you feeling about your life today regarding the narcissist you have or had in your life compared to how you felt when you first started working through the journal? Write about what feels optimistic as you move forward.

_____

_____

_____

_____

_____

_____

_____

_____

_____

_____

_____

_____

_____

_____

_____

_____

_____

Think about a time when you practiced some form of self-care while with the narcissist in your life. Write about how it made you feel. If you can't recall an instance, reflect on something you could have done that would have made you feel better at the time. Let it serve as a reminder of what will help you if you need a self-care moment in the future.

_____

_____

_____

_____

_____

_____

_____

_____

_____

_____

_____

_____

_____

_____

_____

_____

_____

_____

_____

Savoring Simple Pleasures

Savoring is an acute focus on the awareness of pleasure. It's a practice taught in positive psychology that will shift feelings of anxiety to positive emotions.

1. Find something in your space that is enjoyable to you. It can be food, something beautiful to look at or listen to, a lovely fragrance, a picture or souvenir of a memorable time from the past, or an activity that brings you pleasure.

2. Focus on what you choose to savor. Use all your senses in this experience. To lock in the experience of savoring, you can make a quick sketch, express gratitude, and lose yourself in the wonder of the moment.

3. To strengthen the power of savoring, try sharing the experience with a friend.

Let's get back to basics. Are you eating nutritiously? Are you getting regular exercise? Are you sleeping well? Are you keeping up with medical and dental exams? Are you getting rest? Are you staying hydrated? Are you taking vacation time? How are you taking care of your body? How can you improve self-care in this area?

_____

_____

_____

_____

_____

_____

_____

_____

_____

_____

_____

_____

_____

_____

_____

_____

_____

_____

We're here on this planet for a temporary time. We should be spending our time . . . in a spirit of love.

—*Russell Brand*

How are you taking care of your mind? What are you doing to challenge your brain? What do you enjoy learning? What are you interested in reading? Are you watching your thoughts and practicing turning negative self-talk into compassionate self-talk? How are you managing stress? What can you do to improve self-care in this area?

_____

_____

_____

_____

_____

_____

_____

_____

_____

_____

_____

_____

_____

_____

_____

_____

_____

_____

_____

How are you caring for your emotions? Are you connecting to your feelings by naming them? Are you acknowledging your feelings with compassion? Are you noticing when and how you block yourself from feelings? Are you expressing them in helpful ways? Talking through them, writing in a journal, playing music, and creating art are all ways of expressing emotions. How can you improve self-care in this area?

_____

_____

_____

_____

_____

_____

_____

_____

_____

_____

_____

_____

_____

_____

What does spirituality mean to you? How does your experience with religion, or lack thereof, fit into your thoughts about spirituality? What about incorporating mindfulness and meditation? What do you think about gratitude as a spiritual practice? How about yoga, being in nature, or dedicated time for self-reflection? What inspires your spirit? How can you tap into it better?

_____

_____

_____

_____

_____

_____

_____

_____

_____

_____

_____

_____

_____

_____

_____

_____

_____

Take a Mindfulness Pause

Mindfulness is a powerful tool, giving you the power to pause, be present, and break the spell between reacting and responding. As you begin to train in mindfulness, you discover that most human activity is pretty mindless. Think back on some decisions you have made where the outcome would have been different if you had greater mindfulness skills.

Today, take a mindfulness pause. Go outside, unplug from everything, and spend 15 minutes simply using all your senses to experience everything going on around you. Reflect on what you might otherwise not notice.

You can learn mindfulness on your own or through specialized training. There are resources for mindfulness training and organizations that offer classes and retreats in mindfulness. See the Resources section (page 134) for a few suggestions.

What is the condition of your social self-care? How are you tending your relationships? Are you spending time with friends? Are you communicating your needs? Are you practicing compassionate listening (page 81)? Have you identified ways to establish new, healthy relationships? What are activities that nurture and deepen the relationships with the people in your life?

_____

_____

_____

_____

_____

_____

_____

_____

_____

_____

_____

_____

_____

_____

_____

_____

Practical self-care involves tasks to help you avoid future stressful situations. How are you doing with finances, learning needed skills, and organizing your living space? Does thinking about money cause anxiety? How can you get help with this? Have you wanted to take a professional development class? Would it feel good to declutter? What needs attention in this category of self-care?

_____

_____

_____

_____

_____

_____

_____

_____

_____

_____

_____

_____

_____

_____

_____

_____

Identify Your Go-To Distractions

Self-care can be nothing more than looking at your feelings and being curious about them. However, many of us have mastered avoiding unpleasant feelings and we distract ourselves, whether it be with computer games, exercising, eating, drinking, gossiping, internet surfing, sex, binge-watching shows, watching sports, or something else. What are your go-to distractions?

1. Make a list of your typical distractions and choose the four that you do the most often.

2. In the upcoming week, when you find yourself with the urge to engage in your distracting behaviors, pause and explore by asking yourself if there is a feeling you are trying to avoid. Are you afraid of feeling the feeling?

3. Allow yourself a moment to let the feeling bubble up and attend to it somehow. If the feeling is sadness, how can you offer yourself compassion? If the feeling is loneliness, call someone. If the feeling is restlessness, take a walk.

Notice if you are pushing to get things done or make something happen. Think about a recent time when you felt impatient, overwhelmed, or in a hurry. Take a full nurturing deep breath and imagine pausing in the midst of pushing. Recognize the pressure you are putting on yourself, let go, and relax. How does this alter your state of mind? Write a short story about a time you were in a pressured rush. How could you have consciously slowed down and even let go of a "to-do"? Give your story a beginning, middle, and end.

_____

_____

_____

_____

_____

_____

_____

_____

_____

_____

_____

_____

_____

_____

_____

_____

Think about a recent stressful event. How could you have released the stress in the moment? It can help to learn the three Ps: It's not **p**erfect; it's not **p**ermanent; it's not **p**ersonal. Bring to mind the feelings of your stressful event, then think about the situation as you tell yourself the three Ps. Write about how this changes your thoughts about the event and how it lowers your anxiety.

_____

_____

_____

_____

_____

_____

_____

_____

_____

_____

_____

_____

_____

_____

_____

_____

_____

Research has shown that grateful people, for the most part, feel better, exercise more, and have fewer medical issues. A bedtime gratitude practice fosters a state of mind that helps with sleep. Write about what you feel grateful for in the space below. It could be as a small as making it through a long day or as big as successfully finishing a major project. Then consider and write about how practicing gratitude can fit in with your self-care plan.

_____

_____

_____

_____

_____

_____

_____

_____

_____

_____

_____

_____

_____

Make a Date with Self-Care

Today, set a date with yourself for a self-care evening, morning, or day; put it on your calendar; and hold yourself to it like any other appointment. Include details of the event:

I will spend my time _____[insert self-care activity]

I will do this ☐ by myself or ☐ with my friend _____[insert name of friend]

I will unplug for this, and use my phone only to take a selfie during my date.

I'll finish up by choosing my next self-care date and marking the calendar.

Need inspiration? Here are some examples of affordable self-care activities.

→ Create a home spa with bath salts and a candle.

→ Sleep in.

→ Take naps—rest is good for you.

→ Do nothing—set a timer and have no expectations and no technology.

→ Get down on the floor and stretch, just because it feels good.

→ Stare at the sky—watch the sunrise and sunset.

→ Watch it rain or snow.

→ Give yourself an hour of silence.

→ Keep a nice pump bottle of scented lotion next to your bed. Rub some into your feet before you fall asleep.

→ Walk barefoot in the grass.

What is something that would bring you more gratification in your life? What is something that you would regret not doing if you were told you had only a week to live? Reflect on the possibilities, then write about one or more of them here. Include an intention to act on one of these possibilities. Circle back later and write about your experience or progress toward this goal.

_____

_____

_____

_____

_____

_____

_____

_____

_____

_____

_____

_____

_____

_____

_____

_____

I welcome health
and growth in all areas
of my life.

A FINAL WORD

Reflect on all you have discovered about yourself throughout this journal. You are on your way to creating the life you want. With courage and a commitment to healing, you have learned to look deeply inward. Allow yourself to feel a sense of pride for doing this hard work. You can now confidently use the affirmation *I can do hard things!*

The old pattern of looking outside yourself for happiness will continue to be a part of you. However, the new skills you are practicing will become a more natural way of being. Your overall goal is to learn to find joy and happiness within. Just think: 100 days from now, you will be different from how you are today because you'll continue refining your way of living through the work in this journal.

You investigated how you had to adapt to be with a narcissist. You are now unlearning these maladaptive patterns as you create new ways of thinking and responding. Scientific research tells us now that our minds can change. We also know that relational healing can't happen in isolation. By sharing your struggles and what you are learning with a few safe friends, you will create new patterns. You no longer need to spend your energy pleasing others. Be kind to your people and allow them to be kind to you. In your own time, you will increasingly feel the lightness that comes from knowing that you are enough and lovable the way you are. You are learning to protect yourself with boundaries. You are, in a sense, becoming a very good parent to yourself.

It is good to be reminded that it's not the destination; instead, it's the capacity to be present and mindful while on your journey so you can notice the little things and respond to life with a strong sense of self. Breathe deeply, slow down, savor what delights you, and share your uniqueness. Your life is your own. As time goes on, you will feel hurt less often, and when you experience emotional pain, it will feel less intense because of the wisdom and self-compassion you have acquired. You also know how to face conflict and discomfort, and you are now armed with tools to respond in a healthy way. I bow to you, honoring your wisdom in choosing to awaken your authentic self. May you ease your way into more confidence, power, and joy.

RESOURCES

National Domestic Violence Hotline
TheHotline.org
1-800-799-7233
TTY 1-800-787-3224

Anxiety Management

EFT (Tapping—Emotional Freedom
Technique): This mobile app offers a
way to quickly shift your emotional
state. TheTappingSolution.com
/what-is-eft-tapping

Mindfulness Classes and Apps

Calm: Calm.com

Headspace: Headspace.com

Insight Dialogue Community:
InsightDialogue.org

Insight Timer (free): InsightTimer.com

InsightLA: InsightLA.org

MBSR (Mindfulness Based Stress
Reduction): MindfulLeader.org

Self-Compassion: Self-Compassion.org

Smiling Mind (free):
SmilingMind.com.au

Support Groups, Therapy, and Coaching

Co-Dependents Anonymous (very
helpful if you are investigating your
people-pleasing patterns)
CoDA.org

TheLuckiestClub.com

Sobriety meetings

Psychology Today: Find a Therapist
PsychologyToday.com/us/therapists

Queen Beeing
QueenBeeing.com

Will I Ever Be Good Enough?
WillIEverBeGoodEnough.com
/resources/find-a-therapist

Trauma/PTSD

Center for Mind-Body Medicine
CMBM.org/find-a-practitioner

EMDR Institute
EMDR.com/what-is-emdr

Sensorimotor Psychotherapy Institute
SensorimotorPsychotherapy.org
/therapist-directory

Inspirational People

Aiko Bethea: RareCoaching.net

Brené Brown: BreneBrown.com

Dr. Maya Angelou: MayaAngelou.com

Jack Kornfield: JackKornfield.com

James S. Gordon: JamesGordonMD.com

Pema Chodron:
PemaChodronFoundation.org

Books

Complex PTSD: From Surviving to Thriving by Pete Walker

Disarming the Narcissist by Wendy T. Behary

Rethinking Narcissism by Dr. Craig Malikin

The Choice by Edith Eger

The Drama of the Gifted Child by Alice Miller

Unloved Again: Breaking Your Serial Addiction by Elan Golomb, PhD

Will I Ever Be Good Enough? by Karyl McBride

Other

Lifelines is a website offering free workshops, meditations, and community. It was created by a successful businesswoman who struggled with self-awareness and well-being. She now helps others find their way inward. Lifelines.com

Writing to find yourself
JuliaCameronLive.com/the-artists-way

REFERENCES

Behary, Wendy T. *Disarming the Narcissist: Surviving and Thriving with the Self-Absorbed*. Oakland, CA: New Harbinger Publications, 2013.

Brand, Russell. "How To Find Peace? Let Go—Russell Brand The Trews (E359)." Posted July 22, 2015. YouTube video, 9:06. youtube.com /watch?v=67_B8_y6B7w.

Brown, Brené. *I Thought It Was Just Me (But It Isn't): Making the Journey from "What Will People Think?" to "I Am Enough."* New York: Penguin Publishing Group, 2007.

Covey, Stephen R. *The 7 Habits of Highly Effective People: 30th Anniversary Edition*. New York: Simon & Schuster, 2020.

Cuddy, Amy. *Presence: Bringing Your Boldest Self to Your Biggest Challenges*. New York: Little, Brown, 2015.

Desmond, Tim. *The Self-Compassion Skills Workbook: A 14-Day Plan to Transform Your Relationship with Yourself*. New York: W. W. Norton, 2017.

Dyer, Judy. *Empaths and Narcissists: 2 Books in 1*. Independently published, 2020.

Eger, Edith Eva. *The Gift: 12 Lessons to Save Your Life*. New York: Scribner, 2020.

Emmons, Robert A., and Michael E McCullough. "Counting Blessings versus Burdens: An Experimental Investigation of Gratitude and Subjective Well-Being in Daily Life." *Journal of Personality and Social Psychology* 84, no. 2 (2003): 377–389.

Ferriss, Tim. "A person's success in life can be measured by the number of uncomfortable conversations he or she is willing to have." Twitter, January 26, 2015, twitter.com/tferriss /status/559731737992130561.

Fisher, Janina, and Pat Ogden. *Sensorimotor Psychotherapy: Interventions for Trauma and Attachment (Norton Series on Interpersonal Neurobiology)*. New York: W. W. Norton, 2015.

Germer, Christopher, and Kristin Neff. *The Mindful Self-Compassion Workbook: A Proven Way to Accept Yourself, Build Inner Strength, and Thrive*. New York: Guilford Press, 2018.

Gilbert, Elizabeth. *Big Magic: Creative Living Beyond Fear*. New York: Penguin Publishing Group, 2015.

Golomb, Elan. *Trapped in the Mirror*. New York: William Morrow, 2012.

Gordon, James Samuel. *The Transformation: Discovering Wholeness and Healing After Trauma*. New York: HarperOne, 2019.

Hölzel, Britta K., James Carmody, Mark Vangel, Christina Congleton, Sita M. Yerramsetti, Tim Gard, and Sara W. Lazar. "Mindfulness Practice Leads to Increases in Regional Brain Gray Matter Density." *Psychiatry Research* 191, no. 1 (2010): 36–43.

Jaouad, Suleika. CBS News, *Sunday Morning*. February 14, 2021. cbsnews.com/video/suleika-jaouads-journey-between-two-kingdoms.

Kabat-Zinn, Jon. *Full Catastrophe Living: Using the Wisdom of Your Body and Mind to Face Stress, Pain, and Illness*. New York: Bantam Doubleday, 1991.

———. *Meditation Is Not What You Think: Mindfulness and Why It Is So Important*. New York: Hachette Books, 2018.

Katherine, Anne. *Boundaries Where You End and I Begin: How to Recognize and Set Healthy Boundaries*. Center City, MN: Hazelden Publishing, 2010.

Katie, Byron, and Stephen Mitchell. *Loving What Is: Four Questions That Can Change Your Life*. New York: Three Rivers Press, 2003.

Kaur, Rupi. *Home Body*. Kansas City, MO: Andrews McMeel Publishing, 2020.

Kornfield, Jack. *The Wise Heart: A Guide to the Universal Teachings of Buddhist Psychology*. New York: Bantam Books, 2009.

Lamott, Anne. *Almost Everything: Notes on Hope*. New York: Riverhead Books, 2018.

Määttä, Marju, and Satu Uusiautti. "'My Life Felt Like a Cage Without an Exit': Narratives of Childhood Under the Abuse of a Narcissistic Mother." *Early Child Development and Care* 190, no. 7 (2020): 1065–1079.

Malkin, Craig. *Rethinking Narcissism: The Bad—and Surprising Good—About Feeling Special*. New York: Harper Wave, 2015.

McBride, Karyl. *Will I Ever Be Good Enough? Healing the Daughters of Narcissistic Mothers*. New York: Atria Books, 2008.

Miller, Alice. *The Drama of the Gifted Child: The Search for the True Self, Third Edition*. New York: Basic Books, 2008.

National Coalition Against Domestic Violence. "National Statistics." Accessed January 1, 2021. ncadv.org /statistics.

Oprah.com. "The Powerful Lesson Maya Angelou Taught Oprah." October 19, 2011. oprah.com/oprahs-lifeclass/the -powerful-lesson-maya-angelou -taught-oprah-video.

Orth, Ulrich, Richard W. Robins, Laurenz L. Meier, and Rand D. Conger. "Refining the Vulnerability Model of Low Self-Esteem and Depression: Disentangling the Effects of Genuine Self-Esteem and Narcissism." *Journal of Personality and Social Psychology* 110, no. 1 (2016): 133–149.

Ostaseski, Frank. *The Five Invitations: Discovering What Death Can Teach Us About Living Fully*. New York: Flatiron Books, 2017.

Pauketat, Janet V. T. Wesley G. Moons, Jacqueline M. Chen, Diane M. Mackie, and David K. Sherman. "Self-Affirmation and Affective Forecasting: Affirmation Reduces the Anticipated Impact of Negative Events." *Motivation and Emotion* 40, no. 5 (2016): 750–759.

Rashid, Tayyab, and Martin Seligman. *Positive Psychotherapy: Workbook*. New York: Oxford University Press, 2018.

Salzberg, Sharon. *Real Love: The Art of Mindful Connection.* New York: Flatiron Books, 2017.

Seligman, Martin. *Authentic Happiness: Using the New Positive Psychology to Realize Your Potential for Lasting Fulfillment.* New York: Atria Paperbacks, 2011.

Shapiro, Shauna. *Good Morning, I Love You: Mindfulness and Self-Compassion Practices to Rewire Your Brain for Calm, Clarity, and Joy.* Boulder, CO: Sounds True, 2020.

Siegel, Daniel J. *Mindsight: The New Science of Personal Transformation.* New York: Random House, 2010.

Southwick, Steven M., and Dennis S. Charney. *Resilience: The Science of Mastering Life's Greatest Challenges.* Cambridge, UK: Cambridge University Press, 2018.

Toussaint, Loren, Worthington Everett, and David R. Williams. *Forgiveness and Health: Scientific Evidence and Theories Relating Forgiveness to Better Health.* Dordrecht: Springer Netherlands, 2015.

Van der Kolk, Bessel A. *The Body Keeps the Score: Brain, Mind, and Body in the Healing of Trauma.* New York: Penguin Books, 2015.

Van Dyken, Nancy. *Everyday Narcissism: Yours, Mine, and Ours.* Las Vegas: Central Recovery Press, 2017.

Walker, Pete. *Complex PTSD: From Surviving to Thriving: A Guide and Map for Recovering from Childhood Trauma.* Lafayette, CA: An Azure Coyote Book, 2013.

Winnicott, Donald W. "Basis for Self in Body." In *The Collected Works of D. W. Winnicott: Volume 9, 1969–1971,* eds. Lesley Caldwell and Helen Taylor Robinson. New York: Oxford University Press, 2016.

Acknowledgments

I believe that the people who show up in my life are sent to me. They all have meaning. I am grateful for my teachers and healers: romantic partners, therapists, family, employers, friends, and the extended earth community.

I bow deeply to my dear clients who trust me to accompany them on a healing journey. It's a privilege to hold space for your honest vulnerability. Your hard-earned successes demonstrate that the effects of narcissism can be healed.

The voice of my inner child is the heartbeat of this journal. She delights in being heard. I acknowledge and thank her the most.

About the Author

Cynthia Eddings, LMFT lives and works as a psychotherapist in Santa Monica, California and has been an active artist and healer for more than three decades. Her goal is to have an ongoing practice of being at ease with life and she shows up as a safe, supportive therapist for others who strive to be at ease with themselves. In her free time, she enjoys swimming in the ocean, relaxing in the garden, and going on mindfulness retreats. Find her at CynthiaEddings.com.

CPSIA information can be obtained
at www.ICGtesting.com
Printed in the USA
JSHW030204010922
29772JS00001B/1

9 781648 765841